THE LIFE OF
CHRISTOPHER
COLUMBUS

This gift has been
presented to the
Silver Bay Public Library
by:

FRIEND OF THE SILVER BAY

PUBLIC LIBRARY

By
Dr. Nicholas Saunders

W9-ASJ-880

School Specialty
Publishing

Columbus, Ohio

THE CAST

Christopher Columbus *1451–1506. Christopher Columbus was born in Genoa, Italy, to a family of wool weavers. After gaining experience as a sailor, he moved to Lisbon, Portugal, to try to gain support for a new journey he was planning. Backed by the king and queen of Spain, he made four expeditions to find a new route to the Far East, to India, China, Japan, and the Spice Islands, hoping to bring back cargoes of silks and spices.*

Anacaona *Unknown–1503. She was the royal sister of Behechio, the ruler of the Taino kingdom of Xaragua in southwest Hispaniola (modern Haiti). She presented Bartolome Columbus with 14 beautifully carved duho stools. She was married to Chief Caonabo of the neighboring kingdom of Maguana.*

Behechio *Unknown–1502 or 1503. He was the ruler of the Taino kingdom of Xaragua in southwestern Hispaniola (modern Haiti). He welcomed Bartolome Columbus during several visits in 1497, entertaining him with food, music, and dances. He died in 1502 or 1503.*

King Ferdinand *1452–1516. Ferdinand was king of Aragon before marrying Queen Isabella of Castile in 1469. Together, they conquered the kingdom of Granada and ruled over a reunited Spain. Ferdinand was less enthusiastic about Columbus' expeditions than his wife.*

Queen Isabella *1451-1504. Isabella was queen of Castile before marrying King Ferdinand of Aragon in 1469. After conquering Granada, she became queen of a reunited Spain. She was a strong supporter of Columbus' voyages.*

Francisco Roldan *Unknown –1502. Spanish conquistador who sailed to Hispaniola with Columbus but later rebelled against him, bringing insurrection to the island. He cooperated with Francisco de Bobadilla, who had been sent to settle the rebellion, but drowned at sea when his ship wrecked in a hurricane in 1502.*

School Specialty Publishing

Copyright © ticktock Entertainment Ltd. 2006 First published in Great Britain in 2006 by ticktock Media Ltd., Unit 2, Orchard Business Centre, North Farm Road, Tunbridge Wells, Kent, TN2 3XF. This edition published in 2006 by School Specialty Publishing, a member of the School Specialty Family. Send all inquiries to School Specialty Publishing, 8720 Orion Place, Columbus, OH 43240.

Hardback ISBN 0-7696-7416-2   Paperback ISBN 0-7696-4696-4
1 2 3 4 5 6 7 8 9 10 TTM 10 09 08 07 06
Printed in China.

CONTENTS

THE RENAISSANCE

In the 15th century, Europe was changing the world through exploration, trade, and the competition among royal families. In 1492, King Ferdinand and Queen Isabella defeated the last Muslims in Spain and united the country under one crown. The Portuguese were trading with the spice-rich Indies (India and China) by sailing east around southern Africa. Columbus' aim was to discover a quicker westward route to the Indies across the Atlantic. One of the greatest discoveries in history was really an accident.

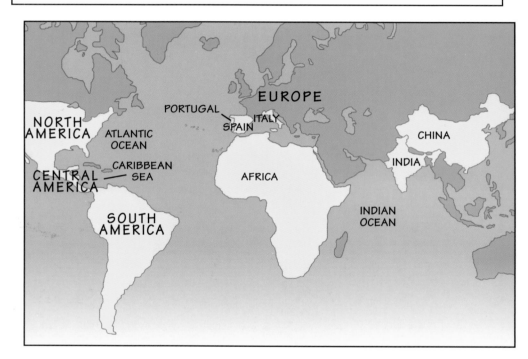

As an adult, Italian-born Columbus moved to Lisbon, Portugal. King Joao II, Portugal's king, did not help the explorer financially.

Colombus' voyages were paid for by the king and queen of Spain.

Columbus' house in Genoa at the medieval Olivella Gate still stands today.

FAST FACT Columbus and other explorers used a medieval navigational instrument, called an *astrolabe*, to chart their locations at sea. It was a flat metal disc that was also used to tell the time by observing the positions of the stars and planets above the horizon.

COLUMBUS' EARLY LIFE

Columbus' birth into a Genoese trading and weaving family provided him a future career in the family business. His own desire, skill, and the era of explorations in which he grew up combined to make him determined to achieve greatness in a changing world.

Genoa, in northern Italy, was one of the most important ports in southern Europe during the 15th century. Ships laden with textiles and spices sailed to and from the port from all over the Mediterranean and beyond.

Weaving was one of Genoa's major industries, and was often run by small family-owned businesses. Both of Christopher Columbus' parents had connections with the profitable trade.

FAST FACT It was common among the middle classes in Genoa for the sons to enter the family business. Christopher and his two younger brothers first followed their parents into the world of weaving and trading.

Christopher Columbus was born between August 25 and October 31, 1451, probably in the house next to the city's Olivella Gate, where his father, Domenico, was warden. His mother, Susanna Fontanarossa, was well-connected to Genoa's business families.

Christopher had a sister, Bianchinetta, and two younger brothers, Bartolome and Diego. Both brothers would become closely involved with their elder brother's expeditions to the Americas.

In the 15th century, Genoa was a major trading center. Its ships sailed across the Mediterranean carrying textiles and wine, and brought back gold, silver, and the spices from Africa and the Orient.

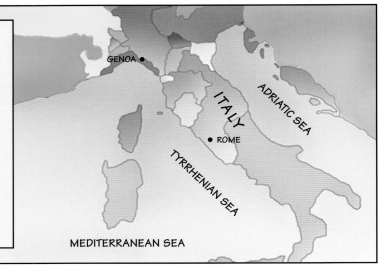

GENOA •

ITALY

ADRIATIC SEA

• ROME

TYRRHENIAN SEA

MEDITERRANEAN SEA

Domenico taught the young Columbus all the mathematical and technical skills necessary to import and export woven textiles and to understand the wine trade into which his father had expanded.

Christopher, I will teach you all there is to know about the family business. One day, you will be a trader like me.

Teach me everything you know, Father.

Besides learning Latin in school, Columbus taught himself other skills that served him well later in life, such as astronomy, geography, geometry, and navigation.

As a young man, Columbus sailed around the Mediterranean pursuing the family's business interests. He sailed to North Africa in 1472, and, a year later, visited the Greek island of Chios, which was an important Genoese trading center.

Chios! The famous island where everything can be bought and sold!

In 1476, after six years of learning his trade, Columbus decided on a more adventurous life. He arrived in Lisbon, Portugal, and began working for Genoese companies trading with northern Europe.

Thank you! It's good to be ashore after my travels at sea.

Welcome to Portugal, Master Columbus. We are glad to see you.

Columbus may have arrived in Portugal by accident. One story tells how he was sailing to England when he was attacked by pirates off the Portuguese coast. He saved himself by swimming six miles to shore and then made his way to Lisbon.

In 1479, Columbus married Felipa Perestrello y Moniz in Lisbon after meeting her in a convent. She was a member of a noble family. Her father had helped the Portuguese king Henry the Navigator gain control of the Madeira Islands.

In the name of Almighty God, I marry you, Chirstopher Columbus, and you, Felipa Perestrello y Moniz.

In 1480, Columbus welcomed the birth of his first son, Diego, but his beloved wife, Felipa, tragically died either in childbirth or soon afterward.

Felipa, my wife. You have given me a wonderful son.

Look, Christopher, how beautiful Diego is!

Columbus grieved over his dead wife and gave her the best funeral he could afford. With the help of her family, he was determined to bring up his son and heir to follow in his footsteps as a trader and explorer.

Oh! My dearest wife, I have lost you too soon. I will raise our son to be a great explorer.

FAST FACT Columbus' marriage, while short-lived, gave him the social respect that he needed in Portugal and Spain to obtain support for an expedition west.

In 1484, Columbus approached the Portuguese king Joao II in his first attempt to gain royal patronage, as well as financial backing, for his expedition.

Welcome, Christopher Columbus! Tells us your plans for exploring the Atlantic Ocean.

Your Majesty, I will be honored to explain everything.

King Joao's experts disagreed with Columbus' geographical calculations concerning the distance he would have to sail before finding land. Columbus was unsuccessful in getting royal support.

In 1485, Columbus left Portugal, having decided instead to ask for support from the Spanish monarchs, King Ferdinand and Queen Isabella.

I must ride to Spain and see if the Spanish king will support me.

Columbus met Queen Isabella and King Ferdinand for the first time in 1486 at Cordoba. He impressed them with the idea that the gold he would discover could pay for a crusade to free the holy city of Jerusalem from the Saracens.

Your majesties, here is my map. It shows how I will discover a new and faster route to the Orient.

We are impressed with your ideas, Columbus. Let our scholars examine your plans. Then, we will give you our decision.

Ferdinand and Isabella paid for Columbus' living expenses in Spain while a commission of experts investigated his proposals. In 1487, they eventually decided that Columbus' geographical calculations were wrong. They refused to support his request.

A year later, in 1488, Columbus met a Spanish woman named Beatriz Enriquez de Arana. Their short-lived romance gave Columbus a second son, Fernando. Although he never married Beatriz, Columbus took care of her financially in later years.

He looks just like his handsome father. I am so proud of our baby son.

Beatriz, my love, you have given me a second wonderful son.

Columbus sent his brother, Bartolome, to seek help from Charles VIII of France and Henry VII of England. Neither monarch was interested.

Columbus turned his attention back to Spain. His driving ambition and powers of persuasion finally gained him the support of two Spanish noblemen, Luis de Santangel and Francesco Pinelli.

Columbus, welcome. My wife, the queen, has persuaded me to give you a second chance to convince us.

Thank you, your majesties. Let me explain in more detail how I will succeed!

In late 1491, Columbus met the Spanish monarchs for a second time, but a month later, their experts again rejected his proposal. As Columbus rode away from court, he was called back and told he could make his voyage after all.

Columbus' supporters had come to a financial arrangement with Ferdinand and Isabella. The monarchs gave their royal permission, but others paid for the expedition.

Christopher Columbus, here are your royal instructions. You will become Admiral of the Ocean Sea and keep ten percent of all the wealth you discover.

FAST FACT Columbus hoped to find a quick route to the spice-rich Orient. He had no idea that America existed. The Spanish monarchs wrote a letter of introduction, which gave their royal greetings to the rulers that Columbus expected to meet in China and Japan.

THE FIRST VOYAGE

Columbus' patience and determination to secure royal patronage and funding had finally paid off. He sailed westward, across the unknown Atlantic Ocean to search for a short and fast route to the Indies, hoping to make his fortune. He left his old life was left behind and changed the world forever.

Columbus' three ships (*Santa Maria*, *Niña*, and *Pinta*) sailed from the Spanish port of Palos on August 3, 1492. There were 90 men on board, including two officials appointed by Ferdinand and Isabella to look after royal interests.

The three ships stopped at the Canary Islands off Africa for food, water, and help to fix the *Pinta's* broken rudder. Afterward, they sailed westward across the Atlantic and into the unknown on September 6, 1742.

Despite promises that sighting birds and whales indicated that land was near, the sailors became worried after several weeks at sea without seeing land. They became increasingly restless and talked of mutiny.

Don't worry, my men! Master Pinzon and I have seen signs of land! The clouds, birds, and flotsam in the water tell us that land is near.

We have been at sea for weeks with no sight of land! We must turn back or die here in the middle of the ocean!

Finally, at 2 A.M. on Friday, October 12, a lookout on the *Niña* shouted that he had seen land. Columbus went ashore, named the island *San Salvador*, and claimed it for the Spanish monarchs. He had unknowingly discovered the Americas.

Land! Land! At last, we have reached the Indies! We must go ashore and greet the people here.

FAST FACT So little was known about the world during Columbus' time that the expedition included an interpreter who spoke Hebrew and Arabic. It was thought that he would be able to translate the languages of anyone the crew might encounter.

Columbus met native Taino Amerindians and noticed their gold nose rings. Although neither could speak each other's language, the Taino exchanged their gold and pearls for Columbus' troops' red hats and glass beads.

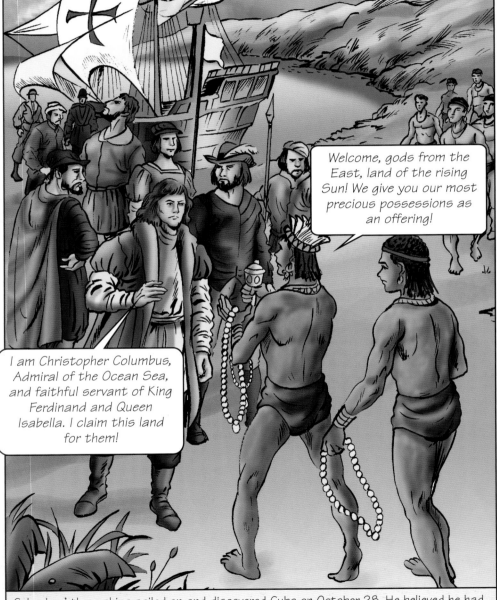

Columbus' three ships sailed on and discovered Cuba on October 28. He believed he had reached China and sent his interpreter ashore with the royal letters from Ferdinand and Isabella. When he didn't find a king, Columbus sailed east.

On December 6, Columbus discovered the Taino island of Bohio, which he called *La Espanola* (Hispaniola). As he stopped in various places, he was told of fierce man-eating people called *Caniba* (cannibals), who terrorized the Taino.

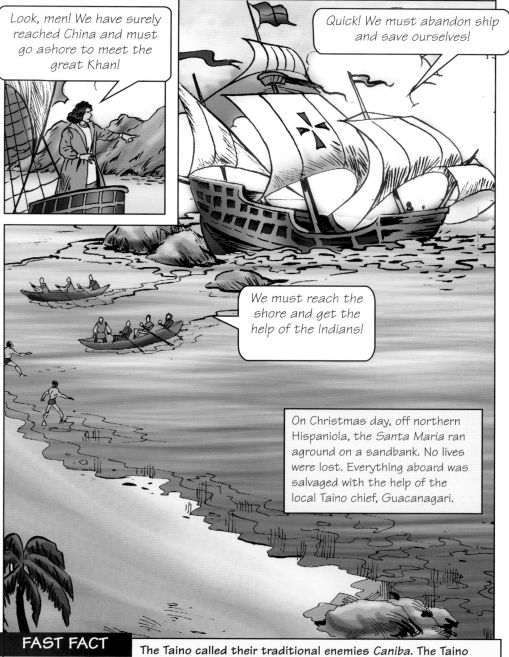

Look, men! We have surely reached China and must go ashore to meet the great Khan!

Quick! We must abandon ship and save ourselves!

We must reach the shore and get the help of the Indians!

On Christmas day, off northern Hispaniola, the *Santa Maria* ran aground on a sandbank. No lives were lost. Everything aboard was salvaged with the help of the local Taino chief, Guacanagari.

FAST FACT   The Taino called their traditional enemies *Caniba*. The Taino accused them of stealing their women and eating human flesh. Ever since, these people, known today as *Caribs*, have suffered from the reputation of their ancestors.

THE FIRST SETTLEMENT

Taino chief Guacanagari entertained the Spanish with a huge feast. Columbus exchanged a pair of gloves and a shirt with him for gold jewelry and a golden mask. Guacanagari told Columbus that the gold-rich land of Cibao lay in the center of the island.

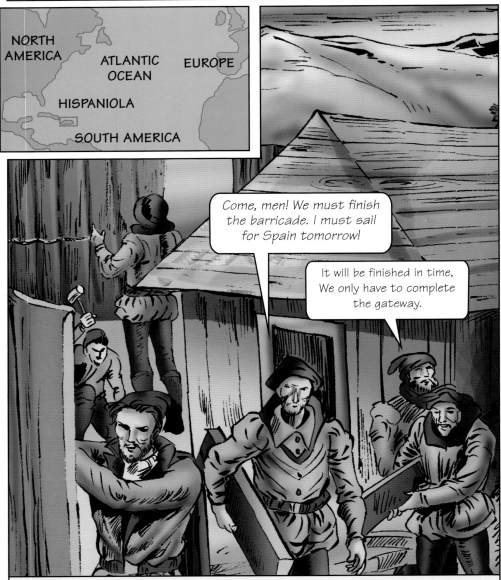

Columbus wanted gold and realized that he did not have enough ships to transport all his men back to Spain. He decided to leave 39 volunteers behind in Hispaniola to search for gold.

Columbus established the first Spanish settlement in the Americas.
His men built the small fortified town of La Navidad near the Taino village.

On January 16, 1493, Columbus' two remaining ships, *Niña* and *Pinta*, sailed out of the bay and returned to Spain. His plan was to return as soon as possible with a larger force and gather the gold that those left behind would find.

Columbus left Hispaniola and sailed across the Atlantic, past the Azores, and then to Portugal, where he met the Portuguese king Joao II. He then sailed to Palos, arriving on March 15, 1493.

Welcome home, Christopher Columbus! Tell us of your astonishing discoveries!

You may stand in our presence, Admiral Columbus. Come and sit by us.

On April 20, Columbus was granted an audience with Ferdinand and Isabella in Barcelona. On arrival, the city greeted him like royalty and congratulated him on his epic voyage.

Your majesties, I have brought great news and wealth to you. I have discovered the westward route to the Indies!

The Spanish monarchs ordered a great reception for Columbus. All of the royal court attended. The Spanish rulers then insisted that he sit beside them. He was later permitted the unique honor of riding through the city alongside the king.

The Spanish monarchs granted Columbus his own coat of arms, a mark of social distinction. They also gave him the privileges they had promised him.

King Ferdinand and Queen Isabella were so impressed with Columbus' report that they granted him permission to undertake a second voyage to the Americas.

Here is our royal permission. You may undertake a second voyage across the ocean.

Thank you, Your Majesty. There is still much to discover.

FAST FACT Unlike the first voyage, Columbus' second expedition was aimed at colonization as well as exploration. His royal permission included instructions that he should treat the Amerindians well, but convert them to Christianity.

THE SECOND VOYAGE

Columbus had discovered new lands for Spain and had been welcomed home as a hero. He now planned a more ambitious expedition that included the colonization of Hispaniola, gold mining, and further exploration of the lands he still considered to be the Indies.

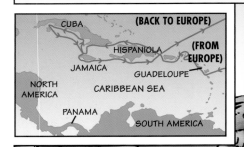

Columbus and his crew sailed from Cadiz on September 25, 1493. They traveled to the island of Guadeloupe. The Spaniards went ashore and investigated a recently abandoned Amerindian village. They saw no natives but observed human bones hanging inside a native house.

The expedition sailed on to Hispaniola. When they arrived, they discovered that La Navidad had been destroyed, and the men left behind to discover gold had been murdered.

La Navidad was not rebuilt and left abandoned. Instead, Columbus founded the new town of La Isabella (named after the Spanish queen) in January 1494. It was built mainly of stone.

Build well, men. La Isabella will be the first Spanish town in this new land. I dedicate it to our generous and merciful queen.

FAST FACT Archaeologists have excavated the site of La Isabella. They discovered the remains of 200 thatched-roof houses and found that Spaniards and Taino were buried alongside each other in the cemetery.

On March 12, Columbus and his soldiers were accompanied by Guacanagari and his warriors on an expedition to search for gold in the interior of the island, where he built the fort of San Tomas.

Admiral, we must also hunt down our men's murderers.

Forward, conquistadors! We will find gold in the mountains of Hispaniola.

On his return to La Isabella, Columbus found many settlers and soldiers had fallen ill and were angry at the lack of gold they had expected.

Instead of solving the problems, Columbus left his brother Diego in charge while he sailed off to explore the coast of Cuba. Columbus still believed that Cuba was Asia, rather than an island.

I must return to Asia and explore its rocky coast. Maybe we will find the great Khan waiting for us.

When Columbus returned to La Isabella, he found his brother Bartolome had recently arrived from Spain with reinforcements. Columbus made Bartolome governor, which angered the settlers, some of whom sailed home to Spain.

Welcome, Bartolome! You have sailed safely across the ocean. Now, I make you governor of Hispaniola!

Thank you, brother. I am glad to be here and eager to see the land you have discovered!

Columbus marshalled his forces, marched inland, and spent a year fighting the Taino tribes of Hispaniola. He was deliberately savage during battles. He meant to intimidate the natives and pacify the island so that it could be colonized by the Spanish.

Charge! Cut down these savages and burn their village. We must conquer the whole island for Ferdinand and Isabella!

A Taino chief, Guarionex, told Columbus that his people knew nothing of gold or gold mining. He offered to feed the Spanish, instead. Columbus refused and built the fort Concepcion de la Vega overlooking Guarionex's village.

In March 1496, Columbus sailed for Spain to defend himself against the accusations of mismanaging Hispaniola made by the settlers who had returned earlier.

When Columbus arrived, he bound himself in chains and pleaded his case to Ferdinand and Isabella.

During Columbus' absence, his brother, Bartolome, put down a rebellion by the Taino tribe, and threw the chief Guarionex in jail. After he was released, Guarionex joined Mayobanex, another Taino chief, but both were captured by Bartolome.

I, Behechio, chief of the Taino of Xaragua and my sister, Anacaona, welcome Bartolome Columbus to our village.

I am honored by your hospitality, Behechio. We will stay with you and discuss how you will pay your tribute.

You will see our great feast, known as areito, and then I shall give you precious gifts.

In January 1497, Bartolome led an expedition to the Taino kingdom of Xaragua in southwestern Hispaniola. He demanded tribute in gold, but when the chief Behechio and his sister Anacaona said they had none, Bartolome accepted cotton and food instead.

A few months later, Bartolome returned to Xaragua to collect his tribute. Behechio and Anacaona entertained him lavishly with a great feast, dances, and music. They then gave Bartolome their tribute of food and cotton.

Anacaona insisted on going aboard a Spanish ship that had anchored nearby to transport the tribute back to La Isabella. She showed Bartolome a great storehouse full of valuable Taino items and gave him gifts, including beautiful clothing, wooden sculptures, and carved and polished wooden seats.

FAST FACT The Taino, Hispaniola's native people were divided into different tribal regions. Their ruling families intermarried with each other. Their tribes maintained political relations by feasting and giving expensive gifts.

THE THIRD VOYAGE

Columbus gained many enemies during his explorations. The Spanish monarchs and government realized that they had given Columbus too much power. They decided the Americas needed to be governed by Spanish officials, not the Columbus family. Columbus was now regarded only as an explorer. He was forbidden to return to Hispaniola.

By 1498, Columbus was back in favor with the Spanish monarchs. They gave him permission to undertake a third voyage that left Spain in May 1498.

On July 31, Columbus' fleet arrived in the southern Caribbean. Columbus christened a newly discovered island Trinidad after he saw three mountain peaks in the distance.

Look there! A new island. I shall call this place Trinidad, after the three mountain peaks and the Holy Trinity.

Columbus led his men ashore on Trinidad's southern coast. They traded with the local Amerindians and gathered fresh food and water before sailing westward.

He sailed past the mouth of the Orinoco River. He realized that its huge flow of fresh water indicated that he had discovered a long-rumored continent, now called *South America*, not another island.

Columbus made landfall in South America on August 4, 1498. The fleet sailed along the coast for weeks and heard stories from local Amerindians about the rich pearl beds further west. They soon reached the island of Margarita. Once there, instead of searching for pearls, Columbus decided to sail north to Hispaniola.

Quick, follow me. We have discovered a great new country. This land is too large to be an island!

FAST FACT Columbus' third voyage was momentous. During the voyage, he discovered the southernmost Caribbean island of Trinidad, the Orinoco River, and South America.

Disobeying Spain's royal command, Columbus arrived at the new capital of Santo Domingo on Hispaniola's south coast on August 31.

At last, I am back in Hispaniola. I must see what has happened during my absence.

Columbus found Hispaniola in the grip of a lawless insurrection led by the renegade soldier Francisco Roldan. The native Taino were rebelling against poor treatment. The Spanish settlers, themselves, were split into factions.

Take this! You natives will work for us as slaves, or else we will kill you all!

Aaaaghhh!

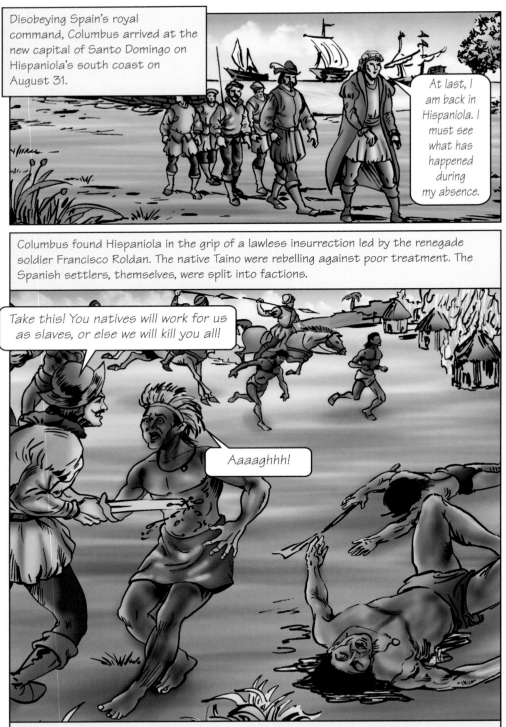

Roldan removed all restrictions against mistreating the Taino. He attacked and burned their villages and treated them like slaves.

Roldan forced the Taino to work in terrible conditions while panning and mining for gold. He had the support of many settlers who had not benefited from Columbus' many promises and frequent absences.

Keep at them, men! If we find gold, we will all be rich!

Work, dogs! Dig for gold!

How did I, Christopher Columbus, Admiral of the Ocean Sea, end up like this?

Columbus appealed to the Spanish monarchs for help, and they sent an official, Francisco de Bobadilla, who had supreme judicial authority. Bobadilla did not like Columbus. When the three Columbus brothers refused to recognize his position, he sent them back to Spain in chains.

FAST FACT European diseases, forced labor in gold mines, and mistreatment all combined to decimate the Taino people of Hispaniola. In less than 30 years, the Taino had disappeared. The Spanish then began to import African slaves to replace the Taino.

Columbus refused to have his chains removed once he was back in Spain. He walked the streets of Cadiz in chains, hoping to gain the sympathy of King Ferdinand and Queen Isabella.

No! I am the one who has suffered at the hands of criminals. They stole the lands that

Look at the great Columbus. He discovered a new world and now walks the streets like a criminal.

I must write to the king and queen to seek their royal favors once more.

At home, Columbus wrote endless letters to the Spanish monarchs, complaining of the injustices he had suffered at the hands of Roldan and Bobadilla. He begged for an audience with them.

In March 1502, Ferdinand and Isabella relented and granted Columbus permission to come to court. Columbus pleaded his case before them. The monarchs decided that he would be allowed one last voyage.

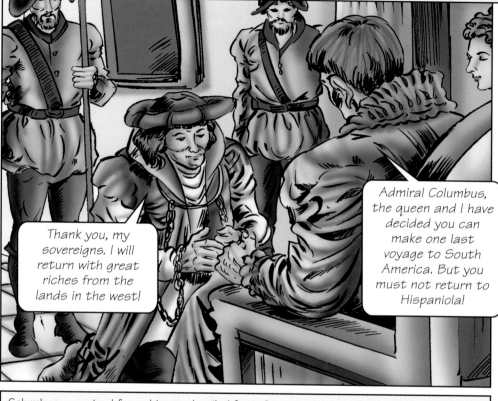

Thank you, my sovereigns. I will return with great riches from the lands in the west!

Admiral Columbus, the queen and I have decided you can make one last voyage to South America. But you must not return to Hispaniola!

Columbus organized four ships and sailed from Spain on May 9, 1504. His brother, Bartolome, and his son, Fernando, accompanied him.

THE FOURTH VOYAGE

Columbus had disobeyed royal orders several times. His original titles and privileges had been revoked, so he had limited authority. Columbus' final voyage was one of exploration. He was stranded on Jamaica for a whole year, and his health began to fail. He returned to Spain but never regained his prestige or influence. He died leaving his disputed inheritance unresolved.

Columbus, stop! The king and queen have ordered that you shall not land on Hispaniola! You must sail on and discover new lands.

Governor Ovando, I will obey your command and leave on the morning tide.

Columbus once again disobeyed his royal orders by sailing to Santo Domingo in Hispaniola on June 29. The new governor, Nicolas de Ovando, refused him permission to land. Columbus then sailed westward to Honduras, Costa Rica, and Panama.

In early 1503, Columbus' small fleet made landfall at the mouth of the Belen River near Veragua in Panama. The Spanish discovered gold during an expedition inland, but attacks from the local Guaymi Amerindians forced them to abandon their discovery.

We have discovered gold. We must mine it as quickly as possible before the natives attack.

Columbus' ships were damaged during the attacks. Columbus decided to return to Hispaniola for shelter. On his way, he encountered a large trading canoe carrying a Maya Amerindian crew who exchanged food and water for glass beads and mirrors.

Bad weather damaged Columbus' ships even more. The ships were blown toward the northern shore of Jamaica. The ships were in such bad condition that Columbus beached them near a Taino Amerindian village.

The Spanish made their stranded ships into houses and traded European trinkets of metal and glass with the local Taino for food and water. Relations between the Spanish and natives deteriorated, however, and food became scarce.

We are stranded here on Jamaica. We must live on our ships until we are rescued.

We must find more wood to finish our building.

Columbus sent two native canoes with Taino and Spanish aboard to seek help from Hispaniola. After a year stranded on Jamaica, the Spanish were rescued and taken to Hispaniola.

We need more food. Offer the savages more glass beads and belt buckles so they will bring us fresh supplies.

Columbus improved the Spanish fortunes when he impressed the Taino by successfully predicting a lunar eclipse on February 29, 1504. The Taino quickly provided more food.

Columbus' health had deteriorated on Jamaica. Though he recovered a little on Hispaniola, he felt he needed to sail back to Spain. He arrived in Spain on November 7, 1504.

Columbus' health worsened while he was in Seville. In May 1505, he felt well enough to visit King Ferdinand. Queen Isabella, his great supporter, had died a few months before. The meeting with the king was not a success.

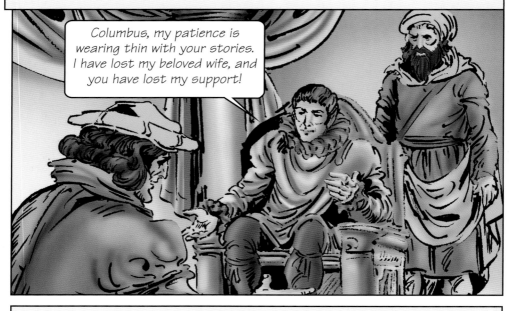

Columbus' condition had not improved when he had an unsuccessful meeting with Queen Isabella's daughter, Juana, and her husband, Felipe. Soon after, he died in the city of Valladolid on May 20, 1506.

Columbus was given a grand funeral and buried in Valladolid's Church of San Francisco. Death did not stop his travels, however, since his body was soon transferred to Seville.

In 1541, Columbus' remains, along with those of his brother, Bartolome, and son, Diego, were transferred across the Atlantic to the cathedral of Santo Domingo on Hispaniola. They stayed there until the French invaded in 1795. His remains were then moved to Cuba.

In 1898, Cuba became independent. Columbus' body was removed once again and taken back to Spain, where he was buried in the cathedral in Seville.

FAST FACT A box with Columbus' name inscribed on it was found in Santo Domingo during repairs to the cathedral in 1877. DNA tests proved that at least some of his remains are in Seville.

TIMELINE OF COLUMBUS' LIFE

Christopher Columbus' life epitomized the Age of Discoveries in which he lived. His life was filled with adventures and world-changing discoveries. His explorations eventually led to the Spanish conquest of the great Aztec and Inca civilizations.

c. 1451: *Columbus is born.*

1472–1476: *Columbus works for his family's weaving and trading business.*

1479: *Columbus marries Felipa Perestrello y Moniz.*

1480: *Columbus' first son, Diego, is born. Felipa dies.*

1485–1486: *Columbus seeks financial backing from Portuguese king Joao II and Spanish monarchs Ferdinand and Isabella.*

November 1488: *Columbus' second son, Fernando, is born to Beatriz Enriquez de Arana.*

January 1492: *Columbus receives royal backing from Ferdinand and Isabella.*

August 3: *He sets sail from Palos, Spain.*

August 12: *Columbus arrives at the Canary Islands.*

October 12: *Columbus makes landfall in the Bahamas, Caribbean.*

October 28: *He discovers Cuba.*

December 6: *He arrives in Hispaniola.*

December 25: *Columbus' flagship,* Santa Maria, *is wrecked.*

December 25: *La Navidad founded on Hispaniola.*

January 16, 1493: *Columbus leaves for Spain.*

March 15: *Columbus arrives at Palos.*

September 25: *Columbus departs Spain on second voyage.*

November 3: *Columbus arrives on Caribbean island of Dominica.*

November 18: *He discovers Puerto Rico.*

November 28: *He finds La Navidad destroyed and its inhabitants massacred.*

April-September 1494: *Columbus explores Cuba and Jamaica.*

March 1495: *He undertakes conquest of Hispaniola for a year.*

March 10, 1496: *Columbus leaves Hispaniola for Spain.*

June 11: *He arrives at Cadiz, Spain.*

May 30, 1498: *Columbus departs on his third expedition.*

July 31: *He arrives in Trinidad and then explores the northern coast of South America.*

August 19: *Columbus arrives in Hispaniola to a rebellion by Spanish soldiers and settlers.*

1498–1500: *He stops the rebellion.*

October 1500: *Columbus is arrested and returned to Spain.*

April 3, 1502: *Columbus departs on his fourth expedition.*

June 15: *Columbus arrives in Martinique, a Caribbean island.*

June 29: *Columbus arrives in Hispaniola but is not permitted ashore.*

May-June 1503: *He explores the Caribbean coast of Central America and Mexico.*

June 1503: *Stranded on Jamaica.*

June 1504: *He is rescued and taken to Hispaniola.*

September 12: *Columbus departs for Spain.*

November 7: *He arrives in Spain.*

May 20, 1506: *Columbus dies in Valladolid.*

1. *Before Columbus, the Vikings had sailed westward to Greenland and landed in Nova Scotia in Canada.*

2. *Geographical knowledge of the world before Columbus' voyages to the Americas was heavily influenced by ancient Greek beliefs. Many believed Earth was flat.*

3. *The Spanish monarchs' list of rewards that Columbus would enjoy if his first voyage was successful are known as the* Santa Fe Capitulations.

4. *Ferdinand and Isabella offered a reward of 10,000 maravedis (coins) to the first person to sight land on Columbus' first voyage. Rodrigo de Triana claimed the prize, but Columbus kept it for himself, saying that he had seen a light in the distance before Rodrigo saw land.*

5. *The place of Columbus' first landfall is still debated. Its native name was* Guanahani. *Columbus called it* San Salvador. *It was changed to* Watlings Island *and then back to* San Salvador.

6. *Despite evidence to the contrary, Columbus never abandoned his belief that he had discovered a quick route to the Orient (China and India), rather than the new continents of the Americas.*

7. *Today, the destruction of La Navidad on*

Hispaniola is still a mystery. It is likely that Taino chief Guacanagari was responsible, but Columbus' need for native ally proved the deciding factor.

8. *Columbus was sensitive to his low social status in Spain. He was proud and protective of the rewards the Spanish monarchs gave him, especially his coat of arms.*

9. *On his second voyage, Columbus took with him Dr. Chanca, his personal physician, and a priest, Father Ramon Pane. Both men wrote rare and valuable accounts of their experiences.*

10. *Columbus' endless troubles on Hispaniola were caused by his arrogant attitude toward the Spanish settlers, his rewarding his family with important positions, and the inflated expectations of wealth by soldiers and colonizers.*

11. *Columbus' epic third voyage led him to discover the continent of South America. He was also on the verge of discovering vast*

pearl beds near Margarita Island.

12. *The site where Columbus was stranded on Jamaica for a year later became the important Spanish settlement of New Seville. It later became an English sugar plantation.*

13. *Columbus' legacy is still debated. For some, he is the great discoverer of the Americas. For others, he is seen as the destroyer of the Amerindian Caribbean, which paved the way for the conquest of the Americas.*

GLOSSARY

Amerindians: *The term given to native people of the Americas. Columbus called them* Indians *in the mistaken belief that he had reached India.*

Areito: *The typical Taino feast and celebrations that included music, singing, dancing.*

Cacique: *The Taino name for a chief.*

Canary Islands: *Group of Spanish-controlled islands 300 miles west of Africa in the Atlantic. The islands were strategically located for voyages west. Columbus stopped there for food and water on each of his four expeditions.*

Cannibalism: *The practice of eating human flesh. Amerindian cannibalism was associated with ancestor worship.*

Caravel: *A small, fast, masted ship. Columbus'* Niña *and* Pinta *were caravels, whereas the larger* Santa Maria *was called a* carrack.

Carib: *One of two major groups of native peoples who inhabited the Caribbean at the time of Columbus' arrival. They occupied the smaller islands of the Lesser Antilles in the eastern Caribbean.*

Caribbean: *The name given to the sea and its islands. Derived from the word* Carib.

Chios: *Greek island that was a Genoese trading center. Columbus visited it in his early years while on family business.*

Conquistadors: *Spanish soldiers who took part in the discovery and conquest of the Americas.*

Cotton: *The kind of material used by the Taino to make clothing, especially for leaders and important individuals.*

Duhos: *Polished-wood stools with a long curving back used by Taino chiefs and shamans.*

Glass beads: *Cheaply made glass beads were much admired by Amerindians, and the Spanish used them to trade for gold and pearls.*

Gold: *For Amerindians, gold was usually mixed with copper and silver to produce the alloy* guanin, *a symbol of sacredness. Europeans, however, were only interested in the pure gold content.*

Guaymi: *A native people of Panama who attacked Columbus when he was searching for gold during his fourth voyage.*

Hispaniola: *The largest Taino island in the Caribbean and the main focus of Spanish conquest and colonization. It was called* La Espanola *by Columbus. Today, it is divided between Haiti (west) and the Dominican Republic (east).*

Khan: The Great Khan *was the name given by Europeans to the ruler of Cathay (China). Columbus was convinced that he would meet Khan during his explorations for a better route to the Orient.*

La Isabella: *First permanent European settlement in the Americas. Built on Hispaniola's northern coast in 1494, it was abandoned in 1497. It was replaced by Santo Domingo on the south coast.*

GLOSSARY

La Navidad: *The first European settlement of any kind built in the Americas. Built in early 1493, it was little more than a few huts and a wooden stockade. Columbus left 39 men here in 1493. When he returned, Columbus found them all dead and La Navidad burned.*

Madeira: *Group of islands, controlled by the Portuguese, located 500 miles off the coast of Portugal. Madeira was used as an advance headquarters for the exploration of the Atlantic.*

Maya: *The main indigenous people of the Yucatan peninsula in Mexico. Columbus intercepted a Maya trading canoe off Honduras during his fourth voyage.*

Orinoco River: *The second largest river in South America. The huge amount of fresh water that flowed into the ocean indicated to Columbus the existence of an unknown continent, later called* South America.

Pearls: *Gems that occur naturally in some varieties of oyster. Pearls were sacred to the Amerindians, and, along with gold, were the earliest precious items traded with the Spanish.*

Saracens: *A name used for an Arab or Muslim during the Crusades.*

Spain: *In 1469, King Ferdinand of Aragon married Queen Isabella of Castile. Modern Spain was created in 1492, when they conquered the last Muslim kingdom of Granada and united the Iberian peninsula.*

Taino: *Formerly known as* Arawaks, *the Taino were one of the two main native tribes that occupied the Caribbean at the time of Columbus' voyages. They inhabited the larger islands of the Greater Antilles in the northern Caribbean.*

Tobacco: *The dried leaves of several related plants that were smoked by Amerindians as cigars and in pipes, often for religious purposes. Columbus brought the first tobacco plant to Europe.*

Xaragua: *Independent Taino kingdom in southwest Hispaniola (modern Haiti). It was ruled by Behechio and his sister Anacaona. Columbus' brother, Bartolome, visited several times in 1497.*

Zemi: *Sacred images of the Taino people. They could be small sculptures, cave paintings, wooden carvings, and textile dolls. They were believed to have magical power, often associated with agricultural fertility.*

INDEX